Edmund Burke

A letter from the Right Honourable Edmund Burke to a noble lord

Edmund Burke

A letter from the Right Honourable Edmund Burke to a noble lord

ISBN/EAN: 9783337108786

Printed in Europe, USA, Canada, Australia, Japan

Cover: Foto ©ninafisch / pixelio.de

More available books at **www.hansebooks.com**

A LETTER

FROM THE RIGHT HONOURABLE

EDMUND BURKE

TO

A NOBLE LORD,

ON THE

ATTACKS MADE UPON HIM AND HIS PENSION,

IN

The Houſe of Lords,

BY

THE DUKE OF BEDFORD

AND THE

EARL OF LAUDERDALE,

Early in the preſent Seſſions of Parliament.

London:

PRINTED FOR J. OWEN, NO. 168, PICCADILLY, AND F. AND C.
RIVINGTON, NO. 62, ST. PAUL'S CHURCH-YARD.

1796.

MY LORD,

I COULD hardly flatter myfelf with the hope, that fo very early in the feafon I fhould have to acknowledge obligations to the Duke of Bedford and to the Earl of Lauderdale. Thefe noble perfons have loft no time in conferring upon me, that fort of honour, which it is alone within their competence, and which it is certainly moft congenial to their nature and their manners to beflow.

To be ill fpoken of, in whatever language they fpeak, by the zealots of the new fect in philofophy and politicks, of which thefe noble perfons think fo charitably, and of which others think fo juftly, to me, is no matter of uneafinefs or furprife. To have incurred the difpleafure of the Duke of Orleans or the Duke of Bedford, to

B   fall

fall under the cenfure of Citizen Briffot or of his friend the Earl of Lauderdale, I ought to confider as proofs, not the leaft fatisfactory, that I have produced fome part of the effect I propofed by my endeavours. I have laboured hard to earn, what the noble Lords are generous enough to pay. Perfonal offence I have given them none. The part they take againft me is from zeal to the caufe. It is well! It is perfectly well! I have to do homage to their juftice. I have to thank the Bedfords and the Lauderdales for having fo faithfully and fo fully acquitted to-wards me whatever arrear of debt was left un-difcharged by the Prieftleys and the Paines.

Some, perhaps, may think them executors in their own wrong: I at leaft have nothing to complain of. They have gone beyond the demands of juftice. They have been (a little perhaps beyond their intention) favourable to me. They have been the means of bring-ing out, by their invectives, the handfome things which Lord Grenville has had the goodnefs and condefcenfion to fay in my be-half. Retired as I am from the world, and from all it's affairs and all it's pleafures, I con-fefs it does kindle, in my nearly extinguifhed feelings,

feelings, a very vivid fatisfaction to be fo attacked and fo commended. It is foothing to
my wounded mind, to be commended by an
able, vigorous, and well informed ftatefman,
and at the very moment when he ftands forth
with a manlinefs and refolution, worthy of himfelf and of his caufe, for the prefervation of the
perfon and government of our Sovereign, and
therein for the fecurity of the laws, the liberties,
the morals, and the lives of his people. To be
in any fair way connected with fuch things, is
indeed a diftinction. No philofophy can make
me above it : no melancholy can deprefs me fo
low, as to make me wholly infenfible to fuch an
honour.

Why will they not let me remain in obfcurity and inaction ? Are they apprehenfive, that
if an atom of me remains, the fect has fomething
to fear ? Muft I be annihilated, left, like old
John Zifca's, my fkin might be made into
a drum, to animate Europe to eternal battle,
againft a tyranny that threatens to overwhelm
all Europe, and all the human race ?

My Lord, it is a fubject of aweful meditation.
Before this of France, the annals of all time

have

have not furnished an instance of a *compleat* revolution. That revolution seems to have extended even to the constitution of the mind of man. It has this of wonderful in it, that it resembles what Lord Verulam says of the operations of nature : It was perfect, not only in all its elements and principles, but in all it's members and it's organs from the very beginning. The moral scheme of France furnishes the only pattern ever known, which they who admire will *inflantly* resemble. It is indeed an inexhaustible repertory of one kind of examples. In my wretched condition, though hardly to be classed with the living, I am not safe from them. They have tygers to fall upon animated strength. They have hyenas to prey upon carcasses. The national menagerie is collected by the first physiologists of the time ; and it is defective in no description of savage nature. They pursue, even such as me, into the obscurest retreats, and haul them before their revolutionary tribunals. Neither sex, nor age—not the sanctuary of the tomb is sacred to them. They have so determined a hatred to all privileged orders, that they deny even to the departed, the sad immunities of the grave. They are not wholly without an object. Their turpitude purveys to their malice ;

and

and they unplumb the dead for bullets to affaf-
finate the living. If all revolutionifts were not
proof againft all caution, I fhould recommend it
to their confideration, that no perfons were ever
known in hiftory, either facred or profane, to
vex the fepulchre, and by their forceries, to call
up the prophetic dead, with any other event,
than the prediction of their own difaftrous fate.'
—" Leave me, oh leave me to repofe !"

In one thing I can excufe the Duke of Bedford for his attack upon me and my mortuary
penfion. He cannot readily comprehend the
tranfaction he condemns. What I have obtained was the fruit of no bargain ; the produc-
tion of no intrigue ; the refult of no compromife ;
the effect of no folicitation. The firft fuggeftion
of it never came from me, mediately or imme-
diately, to his Majefty or any of his Minifters.
It was long known that the inftant my engage-
ments would permit it, and before the heavieft
of all calamities had for ever condemned me to
obfcurity and forrow, I had refolved on a
total retreat. I had executed that defign. I
was entirely out of the way of ferving or of
hurting any ftatefman, or any party, when the
Minifters fo generoufly and fo nobly carried
into

into effect the spontaneous bounty of the Crown. Both descriptions have acted as became them. When I could no longer serve them, the Ministers have considered my situation. When I could no longer hurt them, the revolutionists have trampled on my infirmity. My gratitude, I trust, is equal to the manner in which the benefit was conferred. It came to me indeed, at a time of life, and in a state of mind and body, in which no circumstance of fortune could afford me any real pleasure. But this was no fault in the Royal Donor, or in his Ministers, who were pleased, in acknowledging the merits of an invalid servant of the publick, to assuage the sorrows of a desolate old man.

It would ill become me to boast of any thing. It would as ill become me, thus called upon, to depreciate the value of a long life, spent with unexampled toil in the service of my country. Since the total body of my services, on account of the industry which was shewn in them, and the fairness of my intentions, have obtained the acceptance of my Sovereign, it would be absurd in me to range myself on the side of the Duke of Bedford and the Corresponding Society, or, as far as in me lies, to permit a dispute on the rate at which the authority appointed

by

by *our* Conftitution to eftimate fuch things, has been pleafed to fet them.

Loofe libels ought to be paffed by in filence and contempt. By me they have been fo always. I knew that as long as I remained in publick, I fhould live down the calumnies of malice, and the judgments of ignorance. If I happened to be now and then in the wrong, as who is not, like all other men, I muft bear the confequence of my faults and my miftakes. The libels of the prefent day, are juft of the fame ftuff as the libels of the paft. But they derive an importance from the rank of the perfons they come from, and the gravity of the place where they were uttered. In fome way or other I ought to take fome notice of them. To affert myfelf thus traduced is not vanity or arrogance. It is a demand of juftice; it is a demonftration of gratitude. If I am unworthy, the Minifters are worfe than prodigal. On that hypothefis, I perfectly agree with the Duke of Bedford.

For whatever I have been (I am now no more) I put myfelf on my country. I ought to be allowed a reafonable freedom, becaufe I ftand upon my deliverance; and no culprit ought to plead

plead in irons. Even in the utmoft latitude of defenfive liberty, I wifh to preferve all poffible decorum. Whatever it may be in the eyes of thefe noble perfons themfelves, to me, their fituation calls for the moft profound refpeft. If I fhould happen to trefpafs a little, which I truft I fhall not, let it always be fuppofed, that a confufion of charaſters may produce miftakes; that in the mafquerades of the grand carnival of our age, whimfical adventures happen; odd things are faid and pafs off. If I fhould fail a fingle point in the high refpeft I owe to thofe illuftrious perfons, I cannot be fuppofed to mean the Duke of Bedford and the Earl of Lauderdale of the Houfe of Peers, but the Duke of Bedford and the Earl of Lauderdale of Palace Yard;—The Dukes and Earls of Brentford. There they are on the pavement; there they feem to come nearer to my humble level; and, virtually at leaft, to have waved their high privilege.

Making this proteftation, I refufe all revolutionary tribunals, where men have been put to death for no other reafon, than that they had obtained favours from the Crown. I claim, not the letter, but the fpirit of the old Englifh law, that is, to be tried by my peers. I decline

his

his Grace's jurifdiction as a judge. I challenge the Duke of Bedford as a juror to pafs upon the value of my fervices. Whatever his natural parts may be, I cannot recognize in his few and idle years, the competence to judge of my long and laborious life. If I can help it, he fhall not be on the inqueft of my *quantum meruit*. Poor rich man! He can hardly know any thing of publick induftry in it's exertions, or can eftimate it's compenfations when it's work is done. I have no doubt of his Grace's readinefs in all the calculations of vulgar arithmetick ; but I fhrewdly fufpect, that he is very little ftudied in the theory of moral proportions; and has never learned the Rule of Three in the arithmetick of policy and ftate.

His Grace thinks I have obtained too much. I anfwer, that my exertions, whatever they have been, were fuch as no hopes of pecuniary reward could poffibly excite; and no pecuniary compenfation can poffibly reward them. Between money and fuch fervices, if done by abler men than I am, there is no common principle of comparifon : they are quantities incommenfurable. Money is made for the comfort and convenience of animal life. It cannot be a reward for what, mere animal life muft indeed fuf-

tain,

tain, but never can infpire. With fubmiffion to his Grace, I have not had more than fuffi-cient. As to any noble ufe, I truft I know how to employ, as well as he, a much greater fortune than he poffeffes. In a more confined applica-tion, I certainly ftand in need of every kind of relief and eafement much more than he does. When I fay I have not received more than I de-ferve, is this the language I hold to Majefty? No! Far, very far, from it! Before that prefence, I claim no merit at all. Every thing towards me is favour, and bounty. One ftyle to a gracious benefactor; another to a proud and infulting foe.

His Grace is pleafed to aggravate my guilt, by charging my acceptance of his Majefty's grant as a departure from my ideas, and the fpirit of my conduct with regard to œcono-my. If it be, my ideas of œconomy were falfe and ill founded. But they are the Duke of Bedford's ideas of œconomy I have contradicted, and not my own. If he means to allude to cer-tain bills brought in by me on a meffage from the throne in 1782, I tell him, that there is no-thing in my conduct that can contradict either the letter or the fpirit of thofe acts.—Does he mean the pay-office act? I take it for granted he does not. The act to which he alludes is,

I fuppofe,

I fuppofe, the eftablifhment act. I greatly doubt whether his Grace has ever read the one or the other. The firft of thefe fyftems coft me, with every affiftance which my then fituation gave me, pains incredible. I found an opinion common through all the offices, and general in the pub-lick at large, that it would prove impoffible to reform and methodize the office of Paymafter General. I undertook it, however; and I fuc-ceeded in my undertaking. Whether the mili-tary fervice, or whether the general œconomy of our finances have profited by that act, I leave to thofe who are acquainted with the army, and with the treafury, to judge.

An opinion full as general prevailed alfo at the fame time, that nothing could be done for the re-gulation of the civil-lift eftablifhment. The very attempt to introduce method into it, and any li-mitations to it's fervices, was held abfurd. I had not feen the man, who fo much as fuggeft-ed one œconomical principle, or an œconomical expedient, upon that fubject. Nothing but coarfe amputation, or coarfer taxation, were then talked of, both of them without defign, combination, or the leaft fhadow of principle. Blind and headlong zeal, or factious fury, were the whole contribution brought by the moft

noify

noify on that occafion, towards the fatisfaction of the publick, or the relief of the Crown.

Let me tell my youthful Cenfor, that the neceffities of that time required fomething very different from what others then fuggefted, or what his Grace now conceives. Let me inform him, that it was one of the moft critical periods in our annals.

Aftronomers have fuppofed, that if a certain comet, whofe path interfected the ecliptick, had met the earth in fome (I forget what) fign, it would have whirled us along with it, in it's excentrick courfe, into God knows what regions of heat and cold. Had the portentous comet of the rights of man, (which "from it's horrid hair "fhakes peftilence, and war," and "with fear of "change perplexes Monarchs") had that comet croffed upon us in that internal ftate of England, nothing human could have prevented our being irrefiftibly hurried, out of the highway of heaven, into all the vices, crimes, horrours and miferies of the French revolution.

Happily, France was not then jacobinized. Her hoftility was at a good diftance. We had a limb cut off ; but we preferved the body: We
loft

loft our Colonies; but we kept our Conftitution. There was, indeed, much inteftine heat;
there was a dreadful fermentation. Wild and
favage infurrection quitted the woods, and
prowled about our ftreets in the name of reform. Such was the diftemper of the publick
mind, that there was no madman, in his maddeft
ideas, and maddeft projects, who might not
count upon numbers to fupport his principles
and execute his defigns.

Many of the changes, by a great mifnomer
called parliamentary reforms, went, not in the
intention of all the profeffors and fupporters of
them, undoubtedly, but went in their certain,
and, in my opinion, not very remote effect,
home to the utter deftruction of the Conftitution
of this kingdom. Had they taken place, not
France, but England, would have had the honour
of leading up the death-dance of Democratick Revolution. Other projects, exactly coincident in
time with thofe, ftruck at the very exiftence
of the kingdom under any conftitution. There
are who remember the blind fury of fome, and
the lamentable helpleffnefs of others ; here, a
torpid confufion, from a panic fear of the danger;
there, the fame inaction from a ftupid infenfibi-
lity to it; here, well-wifhers to the mifchief;

there,

there, indifferent lookers-on. At the same time, a fort of National Convention, dubious in its nature, and perilous in its example, nofed Parliament in the very feat of its authority; fat with a fort of fuperintendance over it; and little lefs than dictated to it, not only laws, but the very form and effence of Legiflature itfelf. In Ireland things ran in a ftill more eccentrick courfe. Government was unnerved, confounded, and in a manner fufpended. It's equipoife was totally gone. I do not mean to fpeak difrefpectfully of Lord North. He was a man of admirable parts; of general knowledge; of a verfatile underftanding fitted for every fort of bufinefs; of infinite wit and pleafantry; of a delightful temper; and with a mind moft perfectly difinterefted. But it would be only to degrade myfelf by a weak adulation, and not to honour the memory of a great man, to deny that he wanted fomething of the vigilance, and fpirit of command, that the time required. Indeed, a darknefs, next to the fog of this awful day, loured over the whole region. For a little time the helm appeared abandoned—

Ipfe diem noctemque negat difcernere cœlo
Nec meminiffe viæ mediâ Palinurus in undâ.

At that time I was connected with men of high place in the community. They loved Liberty

berty as much as the Duke of Bedford can do; and they underftood it at leaft as well. Perhaps their politicks, as ufual, took a tincture from their character, and they cultivated what they loved. The Liberty they purfued was a Liberty infeparable from order, from virtue, from morals, and from religion, and was neither hypocritically nor fanatically followed. They did not wifh, that Liberty, in itfelf, one of the firft of bleffings, fhould in it's perverfion become the greateft curfe which could fall upon mankind. To preferve the Conftitution entire, and practically equal to all the great ends of it's formation, not in one fingle part, but in all it's parts, was to them the firft object. Popularity and power they regarded alike. Thefe were with them only different means of obtaining that object; and had no preference over each other in their minds, but as one or the other might afford a furer or a lefs certain profpect of arriving at that end. It is fome confolation to me in the chearlefs gloom, which darkens the evening of my life, that with them I commenced my political career, and never for a moment, in reality, nor in appearance, for any length of time, was fepaiated from their good wifhes and good opinion.

By what accident it matters not, nor upon what defert, but juft then, and in the midft of

that

that hunt of obloquy, which ever has purfued me with a full cry through life, I had obtained a very confiderable degree of publick confidence. I know well enough how equivocal a teft this kind of popular opinion forms of the merit that obtained it. I am no ftranger to the infecurity of it's tenure. I do not boaft of it. It is mentioned, to fhew, not how highly I prize the thing, but my right to value the ufe I made of it. I endeavoured to turn that fhort-lived advantage to myfelf into a permanent benefit to my Country. Far am I from detracting from the merit of fome Gentlemen, out of office or in it, on that occafion. No!—It is not my way to refufe a full and heaped meafure of juftice to the aids that I receive. I have, through life, been willing to give every thing to others; and to referve nothing for myfelf, but the inward confcience, that I had omitted no pains, to difcover, to animate, to difcipline, to direct the abilities of the Country for it's fervice, and to place them in the beft light to improve their age, or to adorn it. This confcience I have. I have never fuppreffed any man; never checked him for a moment in his courfe, by any jealoufy, or by any policy. I was always ready, to the height of my means (and they were always infinitely below my defires) to forward thofe abilities which overpowered my own.

He

He is an ill-furnished undertaker, who has no machinery but his own hands to work with. Poor in my own faculties, I ever thought myself rich in theirs. In that period of difficulty and danger, more especially, I confulted, and fincerely co-operated with men of all parties, who feemed difpofed to the fame ends, or to any main part of them. Nothing, to prevent diforder, was omitted : when it appeared, nothing to fubdue it, was left uncounfelled, nor unexecuted, as far as I could prevail. At the time I fpeak of, and having a momentary lead, fo aided and fo encouraged, and as a feeble inftrument in a mighty hand—I do not fay, I faved my Country; I am fure I did my Country important fervice. There were few, indeed, that did not at that time acknowledge it, and that time was thirteen years ago. It was but one voice, that no man in the kingdom better deferved an honourable pro-vifion fhould be made for him.

So much for my general conduct through the whole of the portentous crifis from 1780 to 1782, and the general fenfe then entertained of that conduct by my country. But my charac-ter, as a reformer, in the particular inftances which the Duke of Bedford refers to, is fo con-nected in principle with my opinions on the hi-deous changes, which have fince barbarized

France,

France, and fpreading thence, threaten the political and moral order of the whole world, that
it feems to demand fomething of a more detail-
ed difcuffion.

My œconomical reforms were not, as his
Grace may think, the fuppreffion of a paltry penfion or employment, more or lefs. Œconomy in
my plans was, as it ought to be, fecondary, fub-
ordinate, inftrumental. I acted on ftate principles. I found a great diftemper in the commonwealth ; and, according to the nature of the
evil and of the object, I treated it. The malady
was deep; it was complicated, in the caufes and
in the fymptoms. Throughout it was full of con-
traindicants. On one hand Government, daily
growing more invidious for an apparent increafe
of the means of ftrength, was every day growing
more contemptible by real weaknefs. Nor was
this diffolution confined to Government com-
monly fo called. It extended to Parliament;
which was lofing not a little in it's dignity
and eftimation, by an opinion of it's not
acting on worthy motives. On the other
hand, the defires of the People, (partly natural and partly infufed into them by art) appeared in fo wild and inconfiderate a manner, with regard to the œconomical object
(for

(for I fet afide for a moment the dreadful tampering with the body of the Conftitution itfelf) that if their petitions had literally been complied with, the State would have been convulfed ; and a gate would have been opened, through which all property might be facked and ravaged. Nothing could have faved the Publick from the mifchiefs of the falfe reform but it's abfurdity; which would foon have brought itfelf, and with it all real reform, into difcredit. This would have left a rankling wound in the hearts of the people who would know they had failed in the accomplifhment of their wifhes, but who, like the reft of mankind in all ages, would impute the blame to any thing rather than to their own proceedings. But there were then perfons in the world, who nourifhed complaint ; and would have been thoroughly difappointed if the people were ever fatisfied. I was not of that humour. I wifhed that they *fhould* be fatisfied. It was my aim to give to the People the fubftance of what I knew they defired, and what I thought was right whether they defired it or not, before it had been modified for them into fenfelefs petitions. I knew that there is a manifeft marked diftinction, which ill men, with ill defigns, or weak men incapable of any defign, will conftantly be confounding, that is, a marked diftinction be-

tween

tween Change and Reformation. The former alters the fubftance of the objects themfelves; and gets rid of all their effential good, as well as of all the accidental evil annexed to them. Change is novelty; and whether it is to operate any one of the effects of reformation at all, or whether it may not contradict the very principle upon which reformation is defired, cannot be certainly known beforehand. Reform is, not a change in the fubftance, or in the primary modification of the object, but a direct application of a remedy to the grievance complained of. So far as that is removed, all is fure. It ftops there; and if it fails, the fubftance which underwent the operation, at the very worft, is but where it was.

All this, in effect, I think, but am not fure, I have faid elfewhere. It cannot at this time be too often repeated; line upon line; precept upon precept; until it comes into the currency of a proverb, *To innovate is not to reform.* The French revolutionifts complained of every thing; they refufed to reform any thing; and they left nothing, no, nothing at all *unchanged.* The confequences are *before* us,—not in remote hiftory; not in future prognoftication: they are about us; they are upon us. They fhake the publick

D 2   fecurity;

fecurity; they menace private enjoyment. They
dwarf the growth of the young; they break the
quiet of the old. If we travel, they ftop our
way. They infeft us in town; they purfue us
to the country. Our bufinefs is interrupted;
our repofe is troubled; our pleafures are fad-
dened; our very ftudies are poifoned and perverted, and knowledge is rendered worfe than
ignorance, by the enormous evils of this dreadful innovation. The revolution harpies of
France, fprung from night and hell, or from that
chaotick anarchy, which generates equivocally
" all monftrous, all prodigious things," cuckoo-
like, adulteroufly lay their eggs, and brood
over, and hatch them in the neft of every neigh-
bouring State. Thefe obfcene harpies, who deck
themfelves, in I know not what divine attributes,
but who in reality are foul and ravenous birds
of prey (both mothers and daughters) flutter
over our heads, and foufe down upon our
tables, and leave nothing unrent, unrifled, un-
ravaged, or unpolluted with the flime of their
filthy offal *.

* Triftius haud illis monftrum, nec fævior ulla
Peftis, & ira Deûm Stygiis fefe extulit undis.
Virginei volucrum vultus; fædiffima ventris
Proluvies; uncæque manus; & pallida femper
Ora fame——

Here

If his Grace can contemplate the refult of this compleat innovation, or, as fome friends of his will call it *reform*, in the whole body of it's folidity and compound mafs, at which, as Hamlet fays, the face of Heaven glows with horrour and indignation, and which, in truth, makes every reflecting mind, and every feeling heart, perfectly thought-fick, without a thorough abhorrence of every thing they fay, and every thing they do, I am amazed at the morbid ftrength, or the natural infirmity of his mind.

It was then not my love, but my hatred to innovation, that produced my Plan of Reform. Without troubling myfelf with the exactnefs of the logical diagram, I confidered them as things fubftantially oppofite. It was to prevent that evil, that I propofed the meafures, which his Grace is pleafed, and I am not forry he is pleafed, to recall to my recollection. I had (what

Here the Poet breaks the line, becaufe he (and that He is Virgil) had not verfe or language to defcribe that monfter even as he had conceived her. Had he lived to our time, he would have been more overpowered with the reality than he was with the imagination. Virgil only knew the horror of the times before him. Had he lived to fee the Revolutionifts and Conftitutionalifts of France, he would have had more horrid and difgufting features of his harpies to defcribe, and more frequent failures in the attempt to defcribe them.

I hope

I hope that Noble Duke will remember in all
his operations) a State to preferve, as well as a
State to reform. I had a People to gratify, but
not to inflame, or to miflead. I do not
claim half the credit for what I did, as for what
I prevented from being done. In that fituation
of the publick mind, I did not undertake, as
was then propofed, to new model the Houfe of
Commons or the Houfe of Lords; or to change
the authority under which any officer of the
Crown acted, who was fuffered at all to exift.
Crown, Lords, Commons, judicial fyftem,
fyftem of adminiftration, exifted as they had
exifted before; and in the mode and manner in
which they had always exifted. My meafures
were, what I then truly ftated them to the
Houfe to be, in their intent, healing and medi-
atorial. A complaint was made of too much
influence in the Houfe of Commons; I reduced it in both Houfes; and I gave my
reafons article by article for every reduction,
and fhewed why I thought it fafe for the
fervice of the State. I heaved the lead every
inch of way I made. A difpofition to expence was complained of; to that I oppofed, not mere retrenchment, but a fyftem of
œconomy, which would make a random expence without plan or forefight, in future not

easily

eafily practicable. I proceeded upon principles
of refearch to put me in poffeffion of my matter; on principles of method to regulate it; and
on principles in the human mind and in civil
affairs to fecure and perpetuate the operation.
I conceived nothing arbitrarily; nor propofed
any thing to be done by the will and pleafure of
others, or my own; but by reafon, and by reafon
only. 1 have ever abhorred, fince the firft dawn
of my underftanding to this it's obfcure twi-
light, all the operations of opinion, fancy, in-
clination, and will, in the affairs of Government, where only a fovereign reafon, paramount
to all forms of legiflation and adminiftration,
fhould dictate. Government is made for the
very purpofe of oppofing that reafon to will and
to caprice, in the reformers or in the reformed,
in the governors or in the governed, in Kings,
in Senates, or in People.

On a careful review, therefore, and analyfis of
all the component parts of the Civil Lift, and
on weighing them each againft other, in order to
make, as much as poffible, all of them a fubject of eftimate (the foundation and corner-
ftone of all regular provident œconomy) it appeared to me evident, that this was impracti-
cable, whilft that part, called the Penfion Lift,

was

was totally diſcretionary in it's amount. For this reaſon, and for this only, I propoſed to reduce it, both in it's groſs quantity, and in it's larger individual proportions, to a certainty: left, if it were left without a *general* limit, it might eat up the Civil Liſt ſervice; if ſuffered to be granted in portions too great for the fund, it might defeat it's own end; and by unlimited allowances to ſome, it might diſable the Crown in means of providing for others. The Penſion Liſt was to be kept as a ſacred fund; but it could not be kept as a conſtant open fund, ſufficient for growing demands, if ſome demands could wholly devour it. The tenour of the Act will ſhew that it regarded the Civil Liſt *only*, the reduction of which to ſome ſort of eſtimate was my great object.

No other of the Crown funds did I meddle with, becauſe they had not the ſame relations. This of the four and a half per cents does his Grace imagine had eſcaped me, or had eſcaped all the men of buſineſs, who acted with me in thoſe regulations? I knew that ſuch a fund exiſted, and that penſions had been always granted on it, before his Grace was born. This fund was full in my eye. It was full in the eyes of thoſe who worked with me. It was left on principle. On principle I did what was then done;

done; and on principle what was left undone was omitted. I did not dare to rob the nation of all funds to reward merit. If I preſſed this point too cloſe, I acted contrary to the avowed principles on which I went. Gentlemen are very fond of quoting me; but if any one thinks it worth his while to know the rules that guided me in my plan of reform, he will read my printed ſpeech on that ſubject; at leaſt what is contained from page 230 to page 241 in the ſecond Volume of the collection which a friend has given himſelf the trouble to make of my publications. Be this as it may, theſe two Bills (though atchieved with the greateſt labour, and management of every ſort, both within and without the Houſe) were only a part, and but a ſmall part, of a very large ſyſtem, comprehending all the objects I ſtated in opening my propoſition, and indeed many more, which I juſt hinted at in my Speech to the Electors of Briſtol, when I was put out of that repreſentation. All theſe, in ſome ſtate or other of forwardneſs, I have long had by me.

But do I juſtify his Majeſty's grace on theſe grounds? I think them the leaſt of my ſervices! The time gave them an occaſional value: What I have done in the way of political œconomy was far from confined to this body of meaſures.

meafures. I did not come into Parliament to con
my leffon. I had earned my penfion before
I fet my foot in St. Stephen's Chapel. I was
prepared and difciplined to this political war-
fare. The firft feffion I fat in Parliament, I
found it neceffary to analyze the whole com-
mercial, financial, conftitutional and foreign interefts of Great Britain and it's Empire. A
great deal was then done; and more, far more
would have been done, if more had been permitted by events. Then in the vigour of my
manhood, my conftitution funk under my labour. Had I then died, (and I feemed to myfelf very near death) I had then earned for thofe
who belonged to me, more than the Duke of
Bedford's ideas of fervice are of power to eftimate.
But in truth, thefe fervices I am called to account for, are not thofe on which I value myfelf
the moft. If I were to call for a reward (which
I have never done) it fhould be for thofe in
which for fourteen years, without intermiffion, I
fhewed the moft induftry, and had the leaft fuccefs; I mean in the affairs of India. They
are thofe on which I value myfelf the moft;
moft for the importance; moft for the labour;
moft for the judgment; moft for conftancy and
perfeverance in the purfuit. Others may value

them

them moſt for the *intention*. In that, ſurely, they are not miſtaken.

Does his Grace think, that they who ad-viſed the Crown to make my retreat eaſy, con-ſidered me only as an œconomiſt ? That, well underſtood, however, is a good deal. If I had not deemed it of ſome value, I ſhould not have made political œconomy an object of my humble ſtudies, from my very early youth to near the end of my ſervice in parliament, even before, (at leaſt to any knowledge of mine) it had employed the thoughts of ſpeculative men in other parts of Europe. At that time, it was ſtill in it's infancy in England, where, in the laſt century, it had it's origin. Great and learned men thought my ſtudies were not wholly thrown away, and deigned to communicate with me now and then on ſome particulars of their immortal works. Something of theſe ſtudies may appear incidentally in ſome of the ear-lieſt things I publiſhed. The Houſe has been witneſs to their effect, and has profited of them more or leſs, for above eight and twenty years.

To their eſtimate I leave the matter. I was not, like his Grace of Bedford, ſwaddled,
and

and rocked, and dandled into a Legiflator;
" *Nitor in adverfum*" is the motto for a man
like me. I poffeffed not one of the qualities,
nor cultivated one of the arts, that recommend
men to the favour and protection of the great.
I was not made for a minion or a tool. As little
did I follow the trade of winning the hearts, by
impofing on the underftandings, of the people,
At every ftep of my progrefs in life (for in every
ftep was I traverfed and oppofed), and at every
turnpike I met, I was obliged to fhew my paff-
port, and again and again to prove my fole iitle
to the honour of being ufeful to my Country, by
a proof that I was not wholly unacquainted with
it's laws, and the whole fyftem of it's interefts both
abroad and at home. Otherwife no rank, no
toleration even, for me. I had no arts, but
manly arts. On them I have ftood, and, pleafe
God, in fpite of the Duke of Bedford and the
Earl of Lauderdale, to the laft gafp will I ftand.

Had his Grace condefcended to enquire
concerning the perfon, whom he has not thought
it below him to reproach, he might have found,
that in the whole courfe of my life, I have never, on any pretence of œconomy, or on any
other pretence, fo much as in a fingle inftance,
ftood between any man and his reward of

service, or his encouragement in useful talent and pursuit, from the highest of those services and pursuits to the lowest. On the contrary I have, on an hundred occasions, exerted myself with singular zeal to forward every man's even tolerable pretensions. I have more than once had good-natured reprehensions from my friends for carrying the matter to something bordering on abuse. This line of conduct, whatever it's merits might be, was partly owing to natural disposition; but I think full as much to reason and principle. I looked on the consideration of publick service, or publick ornament, to be real and very justice: and I ever held, a scanty and penurious justice to partake of the nature of a wrong. I held it to be, in its consequences, the worst œconomy in the world. In saving money, I soon can count up all the good I do; but when by a cold penury, I blast the abilities of a nation, and stunt the growth of it's active energies, the ill I may do is beyond all calculation. Whether it be too much or too little, whatever I have done has been general and systematick. I have never entered into those trifling vexations and oppressive details, that have been falsely, and most ridiculously laid to my charge.

Did

Did I blame the penfions given to Mr. Barré and Mr. Dunning between the propofition and execution of my plan? No! furely, no! Thofe penfions were within my principles. I affert it, thofe gentlemen deferved their penfions, their titles,—all they had; and if more they had, I fhould have been but pleafed the more. They were men of talents; they were men of fervice., I put the profeffion of the law out of the queftion in one of them. It is a fervice that rewards itfelf. But their *publick fervice*, though, from their abilities unqueftionably of more value than mine, in it's quantity and in it's duration was not to be mentioned with it. But I never could drive a hard bargain in my life, concerning any matter whatever; and leaft of all do I know how to haggle and huckfter with merit. Penfion for myfelf I obtained none; nor did I folicit any: Yet I was loaded with hatred for every thing that was with-held, and with obloquy for every thing that was given. I was thus left to fupport the grants of a name ever dear to me, and ever venerable to the world, in favour of thofe, who were no friends of mine or of his, againft the rude attacks of thofe who were at that time friends to the grantees, and their own zealous partizans. I have never heard the Earl of Lauderdale complain of thefe penfions. He finds

nothing

nothing wrong till he comes to me. This is impartiality, in the true modern revolutionary ftyle.

Whatever I did at that time, fo far as it regarded order and œconomy, is ftable and eternal ; as all principles muft be. A particular order of things may be altered ; order itfelf cannot lofe its value. As to other particulars, they are variable by time and by circumftances. Laws of regulation are not fundamental laws. The publick exigencies are the mafters of all fuch laws. They rule the laws, and are not to be ruled by them. They who exercife the legiflative power at the time muft judge.

It may be new to his Grace, but I beg leave to tell him, that mere parfimony is not œconomy. It is feparable in theory from it ; and in fact it may, or it may not, be a *part* of œconomy, according to circumftances. Expence, and great expence, may be an effential part in true œconomy. If parfimony were to be confidered as one of the kinds of that virtue, there is however another and an higher œconomy. Œconomy is a diftributive virtue, and confifts not in faving, but in felection. Parfimony requires no providence, no fagacity, no powers of combination, no comparifon,

parifon, no judgment. Meer inftinct, and that not an inftinct of the nobleft kind, may produce this falfe œconomy in perfection. The other œconomy has larger views. It demands a difcriminating judgment, and a firm fagacious mind. It fhuts one door to impudent importunity, only to open another, and a wider, to unprefuming merit. If none but meritorious fervice or real talent were to be rewarded, this nation has not wanted, and this nation will not want, the means of rewarding all the fervice it ever will receive, and encouraging all the merit it ever will produce. No ftate, fince the foundation of fociety, has been impoverifhed by that fpecies of profufion. Had the œconomy of felection and proportion been at all times obferved, we fhould not now have had an overgrown Duke of Bedford, to opprefs the induftry of humble men, and to limit by the ftandard of his own conceptions, the juftice, the bounty, or, if he pleafes, the charity of the Crown.

His Grace may think as meanly as he will of my deferts in the far greater part of my conduct in life. It is free for him to do fo. There will always be fome difference of opinion in the value of political fervices. But there is one merit of mine, which he, of all men living, ought to be

F   the

the laft to call in queftion. I have fupported with very great zeal, and I am told with fome degree of fuccefs, thofe opinions, or if his Grace likes another expreffion better, thofe old prejudices which buoy up the ponderous mafs of his nobility, wealth, and titles. I have omitted no exertion to prevent him and them from finking to that level, to which the meretricious French faction, his Grace at leaft coquets with, omit no exertion to reduce both. I have done all I could to difcountenance their enquiries into the fortunes of thofe, who hold large portions of wealth without any apparent merit of their own. I have ftrained every nerve to keep the Duke of Bedford in that fituation, which alone makes him my fuperior. Your Lordfhip has been a witnefs of the ufe he makes of that pre-eminence.

But be it, that this is virtue! Be it, that there is virtue in this well felected rigour; yet all virtues are not equally becoming to all men and at all times. There are crimes, undoubtedly, there are crimes, which in all feafons of our exiftence, ought to put a generous antipathy in action; crimes that provoke an indignant juftice, and call forth a warm and animated purfuit. But all things, that concern, what I may call, the preventive police of morality, all things mere-

ly

ly rigid, harſh and cenforial, the antiquated mo-
raliſts, at whofe feet I was brought up, would
not have thought thefe the fitteſt matter to form
the favourite virtues of young men of rank. What
might have been well enough, and have been received with a veneration mixed with awe and
terrour, from an old, fevere, crabbed Cato, would
have wanted fomething of propriety in the young,
Scipios, the ornament of the Roman Nobility, in
the flower of their life. But the times, the morals, the maſters, the fcholars have all under-
gone a thorough revolution. It is a vile illibe-
ral fchool, this new French academy of the *fans
culottes*. There is nothing in it that is fit for a,
Gentleman to learn.

Whatever it's vogue may be, I ſtill flatter
myſelf, that the parents of the growing generation will be fatisfied with what is to be
taught to their children in Weſtminſter, in
Eaton, or in Wincheſter: I ſtill indulge the
hope that no *grown* Gentleman or Nobleman of
our time will think of finifhing at Mr. Thelwall's
lecture whatever may have been left incompleat
at the old Univerfities of his country. I would
give to Lord Grenville and Mr. Pitt for a motto,
what was faid of a Roman Cenfor or Prætor (or

what

what was he), who in virtue of a Senatûs con-
sultum ſhut up certain academies,

"Cludere Ludum Impudentiæ juſſit."

Every honeſt father of a family in the kingdom
will rejoice at the breaking up for the holidays,
and will pray that there may be a very long va-
cation in all ſuch ſchools.

The awful ſtate of the time, and not myſelf or
my own juſtification, is my true object in what I
now write; or in what I ſhall ever write or ſay.
It little ſignifies to the world what becomes of
ſuch things as me, or even as the Duke of Bedford. What I ſay about either of us is nothing
more than a vehicle, as you, my Lord, will ea-
ſily perceive, to convey my ſentiments on matters
far more worthy of your attention. It is when I
ſtick to my apparent firſt ſubject that 1 ought
to apologize, not when I depart from it. 1 therefore muſt beg your Lordſhip's pardon for again
reſuming it after this very ſhort digreſſion;
aſſuring you that I ſhall never altogether loſe
fight of ſuch matter as perſons abler than I am
may turn to ſome profit.

The

The Duke of Bedford conceives, that he is obliged to call the attention of the Houſe of Peers to his Majeſty's grant to me, which he conſiders as exceſſive and out of all bounds.

I know not how it has happened, but it really ſeems, that, whilſt his Grace was meditating his well-conſidered cenſure upon me, he fell into a ſort of ſleep. Homer nods ; and the Duke of Bedford may dream ; and as dreams (even his golden dreams) are apt to be ill-pieced and incongruouſly put together, his Grace preſerved his idea of reproach to *me*, but took the ſubject-matter from the Crown-grants *to his own family.* This is " the ſtuff of which his dreams are made." In that way of putting things together his Grace is perfectly in the right. The grants to the Houſe of Ruſſel were ſo enormous, as not only to outrage œconomy, but even to ſtagger credibility. The Duke of Bedford is the Leviathan among all the creatures of the Crown. He tumbles about his unwieldy bulk ; he plays and frolicks in the ocean of the Royal bounty. Huge as he is, and whilſt " he lies floating many a rood," he is ſtill a creature. His ribs, his fins, his whalebone, his blubber, the very ſpiracles through which he ſpouts a torrent of brine againſt his origin, and covers me all over with the

the fpray,—every thing of him and about him is from the Throne. Is it for *him* to queftion the difpenfation of the Royal favour?

I really am at a lofs to draw any fort of parallel between the publick merits of his Grace, by which he juftifies the grants he holds, and thefe fervices of mine, on the favourable conftruction of which I have obtained what his Grace fo much difapproves. In private life, I have not at all the honour of acquaintance with the noble Duke. But I ought to prefume, and it cofts me nothing to do fo, that he abundantly deferves the efteem and love of all who live with him. But as to publick fervice, why truly it would not be more ridiculous for me to compare myfelf in rank, in fortune, in fplendid defcent, in youth, ftrength, or figure, with the Duke of Bedford, than to make a parallel between his fervices, and my attempts to be ufeful to my country. It would not be grofs adulation, but uncivil irony, to fay, that he has any publick merit of his own to keep alive the idea of the fervices by which his vaft landed Penfions were obtained. My merits, whatever they are, are original and perfonal; his are derivative. It is his anceftor, the original penfioner, that has laid up this inexhauftible fund

of

of merit, which makes his Grace fo very delicate and exceptious about the merit of all other grantees of the Crown. Had he permitted me to remain in quiet, I fhould have faid 'tis his eftate ; that's enough. It is his by law; what have I to do with it or it's hiftory? He would naturally have faid on his fide, 'tis this man's fortune.—He is as good now, as my anceftor was two hundred and fifty years ago. I am a young man with very old penfions; he is an old man with very young penfions,—that's all?

Why will his Grace, by attacking me, force me reluctantly to compare my little merit with that which obtained from the Crown thofe prodigies of profufe donation by which he tramples on the mediocrity of humble and laborious individuals? I would willingly leave him to the Herald's College, which the philofophy of the Sans culottes, (prouder by far than all the Garters, and Norroys and Clarencieux, and Rouge-Dragons that ever pranced in a proceffion of what his friends call ariftocrates and defpots) will abolifh with contumely and fcorn. Thefe hiftorians, recorders, and blazoners of virtues and arms, differ wholly from that other defcription of hiftorians, who never affign any act of politicians to a good motive. Thefe gentle hiftorians, on the contrary,

d̃p

dip their pens in nothing but the milk of human kindnefs. They feek no further for merit than the preamble of a patent, or the infcription on a tomb. With them every man created a peer is firft an hero ready made. They judge of every man's capacity for office by the offices he has filled; and the more offices the more ability. Every General-officer with them is a Marlbo-rough; every Statefman a Burleigh; every Judge a Murray or a Yorke. They, who alive, were laughed at or pitied by all their acquaintance, make as good a figure as the beft of them in the pages of Guillim, Edmonfon, and Collins.

To thefe recorders, fo full of good nature to the great and profperous, I would willingly leave the firft Baron Ruffel, and Earl of Bedford, and the merits of his grants. But the aulnager, the weigher, the meter of grants, will not fuffer us to acquiefce in the judgment of the Prince reign-ing at the time when they were made. They are never good to thofe who earn them. Well then; fince the new grantees have war made on them by the old, and that the word of the So-vereign is not to be taken, let us turn our eyes to hiftory, in which great men have always a pleafure in contemplating the heroic origin of their houfe.

The

The firft peer of the name, the firft pur-
chafer of the grants, was a Mr. Ruffel, a perfon of an ancient gentleman's family raifed
by being a minion of Henry, the Eighth. As
there generally is fome refemblance of character
to create thefe relations, the favourite was in all
likelihood much fuch another as his mafter.
The firft of thofe immoderate grants was not
taken from the antient demefne of the Crown,
but from the recent confifcation of the ancient
nobility of the land. The lion having fucked
the blood of his prey, threw the offal carcafe to
the jackall in waiting. Having tafted once the
food of confifcation, the favourites became fierce
and ravenous. This worthy favourite's firft
grant was from the lay nobility. The fecond, infinitely improving on the enormity of the firft,
was from the plunder of the church. In truth
his Grace is fomewhat excufable for his dif-
like to a grant like mine, not only in its quantity, but in it's kind fo different from his
own.

Mine was from a mild and benevolent fovereign; his from Henry the Eighth.

Mine

Mine had not it's fund in the murder of any innocent perfon of illuftrious rank*, or in the pillage of any body of unoffending men. His grants were from the aggregate and confolidated funds of judgments iniquitoufly legal, and from poffeffions voluntarily furrendered by the lawful proprietors with the gibbet at their door.

The merit of the grantee whom he derives from, was that of being a prompt and greedy inftrument of a *levelling* tyrant, who oppreffed all defcriptions of his people, but who fell with particular fury on every thing that was *great and noble.* Mine has been, in endeavouring to fcreen every man, in every clafs, from oppreffion, and particularly in defending the high and eminent, who in the bad times of confifcating Princes, confifcating chief Governors, or confifcating Demagogues, are the moft expofed to jealoufy, avarice and envy.

The merit of the original grantee of his Grace's penfions, was in giving his hand to the work, and partaking the fpoil with a Prince, who plun-

* See the hiftory of the melancholy cataftrophe of the Duke of Buckingham. Temp. Hen. 8.

dered

dered a part of his national church of his time
and country. Mine was in defending the whole
of the national church of my own time and my
own country, and the whole of the national
churches of all countries, from the principles
and the examples which lead to ecclefiaftical pillage, thence to a contempt of *all* prefcriptive
titles, thence to the pillage of *all* property, and
thence to univerfal defolation.

The merit of the origin of his Grace's fortune
was in being a favourite and chief advifer to a
Prince, who left no liberty to their native country. My endeavour was to obtain liberty for
the municipal country in which I was born, and
for all defcriptions and denominations in it.—
Mine was to fupport with unrelaxing vigilance
every right, every privilege, every franchife, in
this my adopted, my dearer and more compre-
henfive country; and not only to preferve thofe
rights in this chief feat of empire, but in
every nation, in every land, in every climate,
language and religion, in the vaft domain
that ftill is under the protection, and the
larger that was once under the protection, of the
Britifh Crown.

His

His founder's merits were, by arts in which he ſerved his maſter and made his fortune, to bring poverty, wretchedneſs and depopulation on his country. Mine were under a benevolent Prince, in promoting the commerce, manufactures and agriculture of his kingdom; in which his Majeſty ſhews an eminent example, who even in his amuſeménts is a patriot, and in hours of leiſure an improver of his native ſoil.

His founder's merit, was the merit of a gentleman raiſed by the arts of a Court, and the protection of a Wolſey, to the eminence of a great and potent Lord. His merit in that eminence was by inſtigating a tyrant to injuſtice, to provoke a people to rebellion.——— My merit was, to awaken the ſober part of the country, that they might put themſelves on their guard againſt any one potent Lord, or any greater number of potent Lords, or any combination of great leading men of any ſort, if ever they ſhould attempt to proceed in the ſame courſes, but in the reverſe order, that is, by inſtigating a corrupted populace to rebellion, and, through that rebellion, introducing a tyranny yet worſe than the tyranny which his Grace's anceſtor ſupported, and of which he profited in the manner

we

we behold in the defpotifm of Henry the Eighth.

The political merit of the firft penfioner of his Grace's houfe, was that of being concerned as a counfellor of ftate in advifing, and in his perfon executing the conditions of a difho-nourable peace with France ; the furrendering the fortrefs of Boulogne, then our out guard on the Continent. By that furrender, Calais, the key of France, and the bridle in the mouth of that power, was, not many years afterwards, finally loft. My merit has been in refifting the power and pride of France, under any form of it's rule ; but in oppofing it with the greateft zeal and earneftnefs, when that rule appeared in the worft form it could affume; the worft indeed which the prime caufe and principle of all evil could poffibly give it. It was my endeavour by every means to excite a fpirit in the houfe, where I had the honour of a feat, for carrying on with early vigour and decifion, the moft clearly juft and neceffary war, that this or any nation ever carried on ; in order to fave my country from the iron yoke of it's power, and from the more dreadful contagion of its principles; to pre-ferve, while they can be preferved pure and un-tainted, the ancient, inbred integrity, piety,

good

good nature, and good humour of the people of England, from the dreadful peftilence which beginning in France, threatens to lay wafte the whole moral, and in a great degree the whole phyfical world, having done both in the focus of it's moft intenfe malignity.

The labours of his Grace's founder merited the curfes, not loud but deep, of the Commons of England, on whom *he* and his mafter had effected a *compleat Parliamentary Reform*, by making them in their flavery and humiliation, the true and adequate reprefentatives of a debafed, degraded, and undone people. My merits were, in having had an active, though not always an oftentatious fhare, in every one act, without exception, of undifputed conftitutional utility in my time, and in having fupported on all occafions, the authority, the efficiency, and the privileges of the Commons of Great Britain. I ended my fervices by a recorded and fully reafoned affertion on their own journals of their conftitutional rights, and a vindication of their conftitutional conduct. I laboured in all things to merit their inward approbation, and (along with the affiftants of the largeft, the greateft, and beft of my endeavours) I received their free, unbiaffed, publick, and folemn thanks.

Thus

Thus ftands the account of the comparative merits of the Crown grants which compofe the Duke of Bedford's fortune as balanced againft mine. In the name of common fenfe, why fhould the Duke of Bedford think, that none but of the Houfe of Ruffel are entitled to the favour of the Crown? Why fhould he imagine that no King of England has been capable of judging of merit but King Henry the Eighth? Indeed, he will pardon me; he is a little miftaken; all virtue did not end in the firft Earl of Bedford. All difcernment did not lofe it's vifion when his Creator clofed his eyes. Let him remit his rigour on the difproportion between merit and reward in others, and they will make no enquiry into the origin of his fortune. They will regard with much more fatisfaction, as he will contemplate with infinitely more advantage, whatever in his pedigree has been dulcified by an expofure to the influence of heaven in a long flow of generations, from the hard, acidulous, metallick tincture of the fpring. It is little to be doubted, that feveral of his forefathers in that long feries, have degenerated into honour and virtue. Let the Duke of Bedford (I am fure he will) reject with fcorn and horror, the counfels of the lecturers, thofe wicked panders to avarice and ambition, who would tempt him in the trou-

bles

bles of his country, to feek another enormous fortune from the forfeitures of another nobility, and the plunder of another church. Let him (and I truft that yet he will) employ all the energy of his youth, and all the refources of his wealth, to crufh rebellious principles which have no foundation in morals, and rebellious movements, that have no provocation in tyranny.

Then will be forgot the rebellions, which, by a doubtful priority in crime, his anceftor had provoked and extinguifhed. On fuch a conduct in the noble Duke, many of his countrymen might, and with fome excufe might, give way to the enthufiafm of their gratitude, and in the dafhing ftyle of fome of the old declaimers, cry out, that if the fates had found no other way in which they could give a *Duke of Bedford and his opulence as props to a tottering world, then the butchery of the Duke of Buckingham might be tolerated ; it might be regarded even with complacency, whilft in the heir of confifcation they faw the fympathizing comforter of the martyrs, who fuffer under the cruel confifcation of this day ; whilft they beheld with admiration

* At fi non aliam venturo fata Neroni, &c.,

his

his zealous protection of the virtuous and loyal nobility of France, and his manly support of his brethren, the yet standing nobility and gentry of his native land. Then his Grace's merit would be pure and new, and sharp, as fresh from the mint of honour. As he pleased he might reflect honour on his predecessors, or throw it forward on those who were to succeed him. He might be the propagator of the stock of honour, or the root of it, as he thought proper.

Had it pleased God to continue to me the hopes of succession, I should have been, according to my mediocrity, and the mediocrity of the age I live in, a sort of founder of a family; I should have left a son, who, in all the points in which personal merit can be viewed; in science, in erudition, in genius, in taste, in honour, in generosity, in humanity, in every liberal sentiment, and every liberal accomplishment, would not have shewn himself inferior to the Duke of Bedford, or to any of those whom he traces in his line. His Grace very soon would have wanted all plausibility in his attack upon that provision which belonged more to mine than to me. He would soon have supplied every deficiency, and symmetrized every disproportion. It would not have been for that successor to resort to any stag-

H   nant

nant wafting refervoir of merit in me, or in any anceftry. He had in himfelf a falient, living fpring, of generous and manly action. Every day he lived he would have re-purchafed the bounty of the crown, and ten times more, if ten times more he had received. He was made a publick creature; and had no enjoyment whatever, but in the performance of fome duty. At this exigent moment, the lofs of a finifhed man is not eafily fupplied.

But a difpofer whofe power we are little able to refift, and whofe wifdom it behoves us not at all to difpute; has ordained it in another manner, and (whatever my querulous weaknefs might fuggeft) a far better. The ftorm has gone over me; and I lie like one of thofe old oaks which the late hurricane has fcattered about me. I am ftripped of all my honours; I am torn up by the roots, and lie proftrate on the earth! There, and proftrate there, I moft unfeignedly recognize the divine juftice, and in fome degree fubmit to it. But whilft I humble myfelf before God, I do not know that it is forbidden to repel the attacks of unjuft and inconfiderate men. The patience of Job is proverbial. After fome of the convulfive ftruggles of our irritable nature, he fubmitted himfelf, and repented in duft and afhes.

afhes. But even fo, I do not find him blamed for reprehending, and with a confiderable degree of verbal afperity, thofe ill-natured neighbours of his, who vifited his dunghill to read moral, political, and œconomical lectures on his mifery. I am alone. I have none to meet my enemies in the gate. Indeed, my Lord, I greatly deceive myfelf, if in this hard feafon I would give a peck of refufe wheat for all that is called fame and honour in the world. This is the appetite but of a few. It is a luxury; it is a privilege; it is an indulgence for thofe who are at their eafe. But we are all of us made to fhun difgrace, as we are made to fhrink from pain, and poverty, and difeafe. It is an inftinct; and under the direction of reafon, inftinct is always in the right. I live in an inverted order. They who ought to have fucceeded me are gone before me. They who fhould have been to me as pofterity are in the place of anceftors. I owe to the deareft relation (which ever muft fubfift in memory) that act of piety, which he would have performed to me; I owe it to him to fhew that he was not defcended, as the Duke of Bedford would have it, from an unworthy parent.

The Crown has confidered me after long fervice: the Crown has paid the Duke of Bedford by

advance.

advance. He has had a long credit for any service which he may perform hereafter. He is secure, and long may he be secure, in his advance, whether he performs any services or not. But let him take care how he endangers the safety of that Conftitution which fecures his own utility or his own infignificance ; or how he difcourages thofe, who take up, even puny arms, to defend an order of things, which, like the Sun of Hea-ven, fhines alike on the ufeful and the worth-lefs. His grants are engrafted on the public law of Europe, covered with the awful hoar of innumerable ages. They are guarded by the facred rules of prefcription, found in that full treafury of jurifprudence from which the jejunenefs and penury of our municipal law has, by degrees, been enriched and ftrength-ened. This prefcription I had my fhare (a very full fhare) in bringing to it's perfection *, The Duke of Bedford will ftand as long as pre-, fcriptive law endures; as long as the great ftable laws of property, common to us with all civilized nations, are kept in their integrity, and without the fmalleft intermixture of the laws, maxims, principles, or precedents of the Grand Revolution. They are fecure againft

* Sir George Savile's Act, called the *Nullum Tempus* Act.

all

all changes but one. The whole revolutionary fyftem, inflitutes, digeft, code, novels, text, glofs, comment, are, not only not the fame, but they are the very reverfe, and the reverfe fundamentally, of all the laws, on which civil life has hitherto been upheld in all the governments of the world. The learned profeffors of the Rights of Man regard prefcription, not as a title to bar all claim, fet up againft old poffeffion —but they look on prefcription as itfelf a bar againft the poffeffor and proprietor. They hold an immemorial poffeffion to be no more than a long continued, and therefore an aggravated injuftice.

Such are *their* ideas; fuch *their* religion, and fuch *their* law. But as to *our* country and *our* race, as long as the well compacted ftructure of our church and ftate, the fanctuary, the holy of holies of that ancient law, defended by reve-rence, defended by power, a fortrefs at once and a temple*, fhall ftand inviolate on the brow of the Britifh Sion—as long as the Britifh Monarchy, not more limited than fenced by the orders of the State, fhall, like the proud Keep

---

* Templum in modum arcis. Tacitus of the Temple of Jerufalem.

of Windſor, riſing in the majeſty of proportion, and girt with the double belt of it's
kindred and coeval towers, as long as this awful
ſtructure ſhall overſee and guard the ſubjected
land—ſo long the mounds and dykes of the
low, fat, Bedford level will have nothing to
fear from all the pickaxes of all the levellers of
France. As long as our Sovereign Lord the
King, and his faithful ſubjects, the Lords and
Commons of this realm,—the triple cord, which
no man can break; the ſolemn, ſworn, conſtitu-
tional frank-pledge of this nation; the firm gua-
rantees of each others being, and each others
rights; the joint and ſeveral ſecurities, each in
it's place and order, for every kind and every
quality, of property and of dignity—As long
as theſe endure, ſo long the Duke of Bedford
is ſafe: and we are all ſafe together—the high
from the blights of envy and the ſpoliations of
rapacity; the low from the iron hand of oppreſ-
ſion and the inſolent ſpurn of contempt. Amen!
and ſo be it: and ſo it will be,

Dum domus Æneæ Capitoli immobile ſaxum
Accolet; imperiumque pater Romanus habebit.—

But if the rude inroad of Gallick tumult, with
it's ſophiſtical Rights of Man, to falſify the account,

count, and it's fword as a makeweight to throw into the fcale, fhall be introduced into our city by a mifguided populace, fet on by proud great men, themfelves blinded and intoxicated by a frantick ambition, we fhall, all of us, perifh and be overwhelmed in a common ruin. If a great ftorm blow on our coaft, it will caft the whales on the ftrand as well as the periwinkles. His Grace will not furvive the poor grantee he defpifes, no not for a twelvemonth. If the great look for fafety in the fervices they render to this Gallick caufe, it is to be foolifh, even above the weight of privilege allowed to wealth. If his Grace be one of thefe whom they endeavour to profelytize, he ought to be aware of the character of the feft, whofe doftrines he is invited to embrace. With them, infurreftion is the moft facred of revolutionary duties to the ftate. Ingratitude to benefactors is the firft of revolutionary virtues. Ingratitude is indeed their four cardinal virtues compafted and amalgamated into one ; and he will find it in every thing that has happened fince the commencement of the philofophick revolution to this hour. If he pleads the merit of having performed the duty of infurreftion againft the order he lives in (God forbid he ever fhould), the merit of others will

will be to perform the duty of infurrection againft him. If he pleads (again God forbid he fhould, and I do not fufpect he will) his
ingratitude to the Crown for it's creation of his
family, others will plead their right and duty
to pay him in kind. They will laugh, indeed
they will laugh, at his parchment and his wax.
His deeds will be drawn out with the reft of
the lumber of his evidence room, and burnt to
the tune of *ça ira* in the courts of Bedford (then
Equality) Houfe.

Am I to blame, if I attempt to pay his Grace's
hoftile reproaches to me with a friendly admoni-
tion to himfelf? Can I be blamed, for pointing out
to him in what manner he is like to be affected,
if the fect of the cannibal philofophers of
France fhould profelytize any confiderable part
of this people, and, by their joint profelytizing
arms, fhould conquer that Government, to
which his Grace does not feem to me to give all
the fupport his own fecurity demands? Surely
it is proper, that he, and that others like him,
fhould know the true genius of this fect; what
their opinions are; what they have done: and
to whom; and what, (if a prognoftick is to be
formed from the difpofitions and actions of
men) it is certain they will do hereafter. He
ought

ought to know, that they have fworn affiftance, the only engagement they ever will keep, to all in this country, who bear a refemblance to themfelves, and who think as fuch, that *The whole duty of man* confifts in deftruction. They are a mifallied and difparaged branch of the houfe of Nimrod. They are the Duke of Bedford's natural hunters; and he is their natural game. Becaufe he is not very profoundly reflecting, he fleeps in profound fecurity: they, on the contrary, are always vigilant, active, enterprizing, and though far removed from any knowledge, which makes men eftimable or ufeful, in all the inftruments and refources of evil; their leaders are not meanly inftructed, or infufficiently furnifhed. In the French Revolution every thing is new; and, from want of preparation to meet fo unlooked for an evil, every thing is dangerous. Never, before this time, was a fet of literary men, converted into a gang of robbers and affaffins. Never before, did a den of bravoes and banditti, affume the garb and tone of an academy of philofophers.

Let me tell his Grace, that an union of fuch characters, monftrous as it feems, is not made for producing defpicable enemies. But if they are formidable as foes, as friends they are

I

dreadful

dreadful indeed. The men of property in France confiding in a force, which seemed to be irresistible, because it had never been tried, neglected to prepare for a conflict with their enemies at their own weapons. They were found in such a situation as the Mexicans were, when they were attacked by the dogs, the cavalry, the iron, and the gunpowder of an handful of bearded men, whom they did not know to exist in nature. This is a comparison that some, I think, have made; and it is just. In France they had their enemies within their houses. They were even in the bosoms of many of them. But they had not sagacity to discern their savage character. They seemed tame, and even caressing. They had nothing but *douce humanité* in their mouth. They could not bear the punishment of the mildest laws on the greatest criminals. The slightest severity of justice made their flesh creep. The very idea that war existed in the world disturbed their repose. Military glory was no more, with them, than a splendid infamy. Hardly would they hear of self defence, which they reduced within such bounds, as to leave it no defence at all. All this while they meditated the confiscations and massacres we have seen. Had any one told these unfortunate Noblemen and Gentlemen, how, and

by

by whom, the grand fabrick of the French monarchy under which they flourifhed would be
fubverted, they would not have pitied him as a
vifionary, but would have turned from him as
what they call a *mauvais plaifant.* Yet we have
feen what has happened. The perfons who
have fuffered from the cannibal philofophy of
France, are fo like the Duke of Bedford,
that nothing but his Grace's probably not
fpeaking quite fo good French, could enable us
to find out any difference. A great many of
them had as pompous titles as he, and were of
full as illuftrious a race : fome few of them had
fortunes as ample; feveral of them, without
meaning the leaft difparagement to the Duke of
Bedford, were as wife, and as virtuous, and as
valiant, and as well educated, and as compleat in
all the lineaments of men of honour as he is :
And to all this they had added the powerful
outguard of a military profeffion, which, in it's
nature, renders men fomewhat more cautious
than thofe, who have nothing to attend to
but the lazy enjoyment of undifturbed poffeffions. But fecurity was their ruin. They are
dafhed to pieces in the ftorm, and our fhores
are covered with the wrecks. If they had
been aware that fuch a thing might happen,
fuch a thing never could have happened.

I assure his Grace, that if I state to him the designs of his enemies, in a manner which may appear to him ludicrous and impossible, I tell him nothing that has not exactly happened, point by point, but twenty-four mile from our own shore. I assure him that the Frenchified faction, more encouraged, than others are warned, by what has happened in France, look at him and his landed possessions, as an object at once of curiosity and rapacity. He is made for them in every part of their double character. As robbers, to them he is a noble booty: as speculatists, he is a glorious subject for their experimental philosophy. He affords matter for an extensive analysis, in all the branches of their science, geometrical, physical, civil and political. These philosophers are fanaticks; independent of any interest, which if it operated alone would make them much more tractable, they are carried with such an headlong rage towards every desperate trial, that they would sacrifice the whole human race to the slighteft of their experiments. I am better able to enter into the character of this description of men than the noble Duke can be. I have lived long and variously in the World. Without any considerable pretensions to literature in myself, I have aspired.

to

to the love of letters. I have lived for a great
many years in habitudes with thofe who profef-
fed them. I can form a tolerable eftimate of
what is likely to happen from a character,
chiefly dependent for fame and fortune, on
knowledge and talent, as well in it's morbid
and perverted ftate, as in that which is found
and natural. Naturally men fo formed and
finifhed are the firft gifts of Providence to the
World. But when they have once thrown off the
fear of God, which was in all ages too often the
cafe, and the fear of man, which is now the cafe,
and when in that ftate they come to underftand
one another, and to act in corps, a more dreadful
calamity cannot arife out of Hell to fcourge
mankind. Nothing can be conceived more
hard than the heart of a thorough-bred meta-
phyfician. It comes nearer to the cold malignity of a wicked fpirit than to the frailty and
paffion of a man. It is like that of the principle of Evil himfelf, incorporeal, pure, un-
mixed, dephlegmated, defecated evil. It is no
eafy operation to eradicate humanity from the
human breaft. What Shakefpeare calls " the
compunctious vifitings of nature," will fome-
times knock at their hearts, and proteft againft
their murderous fpeculations. But they have
a means of compounding with their nature.

Their

Their humanity. is. not diffolved. They. only
give it a long prorogation. They are ready to
declare, that they do not think two thoufand
years too long a period for the good that they
purfue. It is remarkable, that they never fee
any way to their projected good but by the road
of fome evil. Their imagination is not fatigued,
with the contemplation of human fuffering thro'
the wild wafte of centuries added to centuries,
of mifery and defolation. Their humanity is at
their horizon—and, like the horizon, it always
flies before them. The geometricians, and
the chymifts bring, the one from the dry
bones of their diagrams, and the other from
the foot of their furnaces, difpofitions that
make them worfe than indifferent about thofe
feelings and habitudes, which are the fupports
of the moral world. Ambition is come upon
them fuddenly; they are intoxicated with it,
and it has rendered them fearlefs of the danger, which may from thence arife to others
or to themfelves. Thefe philofophers, confider men in their experiments, no more than
they do mice in an air pump, or in a recipient
of mephitick gas. Whatever his Grace may think
of himfelf, they look upon him, and every thing
that belongs to him, with no more regard than
they do upon the whifkers of that little long-
tailed

tailed animal, that has been long the game of the grave, demure, infidious, fpring-nailed, velvet-pawed, green-eyed philofophers, whether going upon two legs, or upon four.

His Grace's landed poffeffions are irrefiftibly inviting to an *agrarian* experiment. They are a downright infult upon the Rights of Man. They are more extenfive than the territory of many of the Grecian republicks; and they are without comparifon more fertile than moft of them. There are now republicks in Italy, in Germany and in Swifferland, which do not pof-fefs any thing like fo fair and ample a domain. There is fcope for feven philofophers to proceed in their analytical experiments, upon Harington's feven different forms of republicks, in the acres of this one Duke. Hitherto they have been wholly unproductive to fpeculation; fitted for nothing but to fatten bullocks, and to produce grain for beer, ftill more to ftupify the dull Englifh underftanding. Abbé Sieyes has whole nefts of pigeon-holes full of conftitutions ready made, ticketed, forted, and numbered; fuited to every feafon and every fancy; fome with the top of the pattern at the bottom, and fome with the bottom at the top; fome plain, fome flowered; fome diftinguifhed for their fimplicity;

fimplicity; others for their complexity; fome
of blood colour; fome of *boue de Paris*; fome
with directories, others without a direction;
fome with councils of elders, and councils of
youngfters; fome without any council at all.
Some where the electors choofe the reprefentatives ; others, where the reprefentatives choofe
the electors. Some in long coats, and fome in
fhort cloaks; fome with ; antaloons; fome without breeches. Some with five fhilling qualifica-
tions; fome totally unqualified. So that no con-
ftitution-fancier may go unfuited from his fhop,
provided he loves a pattern of pillage, oppreffion,
arbitrary imprifonment, confifcation, exile, revolutionary judgment, and legalifed premeditated
murder, in any fhapes into which they can be
put. What a pity it is, that the progrefs of experimental philofophy fhould be checked by his
Grace's monopoly! Such are their fentiments,
I affure him; fuch is their language when they
dare to fpeak ; and fuch are their proceedings,
when they have the means to act.

Their geographers, and geometricians, have
been fome time out of practice. It is fome time
fince they have divided their own country into
fquares. That figure has loft the charms of it's
novelty.

the oldeſt and pureſt nobility that Europe can boaſt, among a people nenowned above all others for love of their native land. Though it was never ſhewn in inſult to any human being, Lord Kepple was ſomething high. It was a wild ſtock of pride, on which the tendereſt of all hearts had grafted the milder virtues. He valued ancient nobility; and he was not diſinclined to augment it with new honours. He valued the old nobility and the new, not as an excuſe for inglorious ſloth, but as an incitement to virtuous activity. He conſidered it as a ſort of cure for ſelfiſhneſs and a narrow mind; conceiving that a man born in an elevated place, in himſelf was nothing, but every thing in what went before, and what was to come after him. Without much ſpeculation, but by the ſure inſtinct of ingenuous feelings, and by the dictates of plain unſophiſticated natural underſtanding, he felt, that no great Commonwealth could by any poſſibility long ſubſiſt, without a body of ſome · kind or other of nobility, decorated with honour, and fortified by privilege. This nobility forms the chain that connects the ages of a nation, which otherwiſe (with Mr. Paine) would ſoon be taught that no one generation can bind another. He felt that no political fabrick could be well made without ſome ſuch order of things

L   as

as might, through a series of time, afford a rational hope of securing unity, coherence, consistency, and stability to the state. He felt that nothing else can protect it against the levity of courts, and the greater levity of the multitude. That to talk of hereditary monarchy without any thing else of hereditary reverence in the Commonwealth, was a low-minded absurdity; fit only for those detestable " fools aspiring to be knaves," who began to forge in 1789, the false money of the French Constitution—That it is one fatal objection to all *new* fancied and *new fabricated* Republicks, (among a people, who, once possessing such an advantage, have wickedly and insolently rejected it,) that the *prejudice* of an old nobility is a thing that *cannot* be made. It may be improved, it may be corrected, it may be replenished: men may be taken from it, or aggregated to it, but the *thing itself* is matter of *inveterate* opinion, and therefore *cannot* be matter of mere positive institution. He felt, that this nobility, in fact does not exist in wrong of other orders of the state, but by them, and for them.

I knew the man I speak of; and, if we can divine the future, out of what we collect from the past, no person living would look with more

scorn

scorn and horrour on the impious parricide committed on all their anceftry, and on the defperate attainder paffed on all their pofterity, by the Orleans, and the Rochefoucaults, and the Fayettes, and the Vifcomtes de Noailles, and ' the falfe Perigords, and the long *et cætera* of the perfidious Sans Culottes of the court, who like demoniacks, poffeffed with a fpirit of fallen pride, and inverted ambition, abdicated their dignities, difowned their families, betrayed the moft facred of all trufts, and by breaking to pieces a great link of fociety, and all the cramps and holdings of the ftate, brought eternal confufion and defolation on their country. For the fate of the mifcreant parricides themfelves he would have had no pity. Compaffion for the myriads of men, of whom the world was not worthy, who by their means have perifhed in prifons, or on fcaffolds, or are pining in beggary and exile, would leave no room in his, or in any well-formed mind, for any fuch fenfation. We are not made at once to pity the oppreffor and the oppreffed.

Looking to his Batavian defcent, how could he bear to behold his kindred, the defcendants of the brave nobility of Holland, whofe blood prodigally poured out, had, more than all the ca-

nals,

nals, meers, and inundations of their country, protected their independence, to behold them bowed in the bafeft fervitude, to the bafeft and vileft of the human race; in fervitude to thofe who in no refpect, were fuperior in dignity, or could afpire to a better 'place than that of hangmen to the tyrants, to whofe fceptered pride they had oppofed an elevation of foul, that furmounted, and overpowered the loftinefs of Caftile, the haughtinefs of Auftria, and the overbearing arrogance of France?

Could he with patience bear, that the children of that nobility, who would have deluged their country and given it to the fea, rather than fubmit to Louis XIV. who was then in his meridian glory, when his arms were conducted by the Turennes, by the Luxembourgs, by the Boufflers; when his councils were directed by the Colberts, and the Louvois; when his tribunals were filled by the Lamoignons and the DaguclTaus---that thefe fhould be given up to the cruel fport of the Pichegru's, the Jourdans, the Santerres, under the Rollands, and Briffots, and Gorfas, and Robefpierres, the Reubels, the Carnots, and Talliens, and Dantons, and the whole tribe of Regicides, robbers, and revolutionary judges, that, from the rotten carcafe of

their

their own murdered country, have poured out innumerable fwarms of the loweft, and at once the moft deftructive of the claffes of animated nature, which like columns of locufts, have laid wafte the faireft part of the world?

Would Kepple have borne to fee the ruin of the virtuous Patricians, that happy union of the noble and the burgher, who with fignal prudence and integrity, had long governed the cities of the confederate Republick, the cherifhing fathers of their country, who, denying commerce to them-felves, made it flourifh in a manner unexampled under their protection? Could Kepple have borne that a vile faction fhould totally deftroy this harmonious conftruction, in favour of a robbing Democracy, founded on the fpurious rights of man?

He was no great clerk, but he was perfectly well verfed in the interefts of Europe, and he could not have heard with patience, that the country of Grotius, the cradle of the Law of Nations, and one of the richeft repofitories of all Law, fhould be taught a new code by the ignorant flippancy of Thomas Paine, the pre-fumptuous foppery of La Fayette, with his ftolen rights of man in his hand, the wild profligate intrigue

intrigue and turbulency of Marat, and the impious sophistry of Condorcet, in his insolent addresses to the Batavian Republick?

Could Keppel, who idolized the house of Nassau, who was himself given to England, along with the blessings of the British and Dutch revolutions; with revolutions of stability; with revolutions which consolidated and married the liberties and the interests of the two nations for ever, could he see the fountain of British liberty itself in servitude to France? Could he see with patience a Prince of Orange expelled as a sort of diminutive despot, with every kind of contumely, from the country, which that family of deliverers had so often rescued from slavery, and obliged to live in exile in another country, which owes it's liberty to his house?

Would Keppel have heard with patience, that the conduct to be held on such occasions was to become short by the knees to the faction of the homicides, to intreat them quietly to retire? or if the fortune of war should drive them from their first wicked and unprovoked invasion, that no security should be taken, no arrangement made, no barrier formed, no alliance entered into for the security of that, which under a foreign

reign name is the moft precious part of England? What would he have faid, if it was even propofed that the Auftrian Netherlands (which ought to be a barrier to Holland, and the tie of an alliance, to protect her againft any fpecies of rule that might be erected, or even be reftored in France) fhould be formed into a republick under her influence and dependent upon her power?

But above all, what would he have faid, if he had heard it made a matter of accufation againft me, by his nephew the Duke of Bedford, that I was the author of the war? Had I a mind to keep that high diftinction to myfelf, as from pride I might, but from juftice I dare not, he would have fnatched his fhare of it from my hand, and held it with the grafp of a dying convulfion to his end.

It would be a moft arrogant prefumption in me to affume to myfelf the glory of what belongs to his Majefty, and to his Minifters, and to his Parliament, and to the far greater majority of his faithful people: But had I ftood alone to counfel, and that all were determined to be guided by my advice, and to follow it implicitly—then I fhould have been the fole author of a war. But it fhould have been a war on

my